GOSH!!! I'M IN LOVE WITH AN ADDICT: A STEP BY STEP GUIDE ON HOW TO DEAL WITH AN ADDICTED PARTNER

Lauren C. Oaks

Table of contents

Chapter 1:UNDERSTANDING ADDICTION

What Is Addiction?

Addiction is a persistent, backsliding mind illness characterized by a physical and mental reliance on drugs, liquor, or a way of behaving. An individual with an addiction will frequently seek after their poisonous propensities notwithstanding placing themselves or others in danger.

An addiction vigorously influences how an individual thinks, feels, and acts. Numerous people with habit issues know they have an issue yet experience issues halting all alone. While it tends to be enticing to attempt a drug or habit-forming movement interestingly, it's very much simple for things to go south — particularly on account of the drug and liquor misuse. Individuals foster resilience when they more than once misuse substances over the long run. That implies bigger measures of drug or liquor are expected to accomplish the ideal impacts, raising the idea of dependence.

Delayed substance misuse can bring about a hazardous pattern of dependence: one where individuals need to keep involving drugs or liquor to stay away from the awkward side effects of withdrawal. When individuals acknowledge they have an issue drug or liquor might have previously held onto control, making addicts focus on substance maltreatment over all the other things that were once significant in their lives.

Nobody at any point intends to become dependent. There are innumerable motivations behind why somebody would attempt a substance or conduct. Some are driven by interest and companion pressure, while others are searching for a method for easing pressure. Youngsters who experience childhood in conditions where drug and liquor are available have a more serious gamble of fostering a substance use jumble not too far off.

Perceiving And Understanding Addiction

Distinguishing a substance use disorder can be a convoluted cycle. While certain indications of habit are self-evident, others are more challenging to perceive. Many individuals who acknowledge they have an issue will endeavor to cover it from friends and family, making it harder to tell whether someone is engaging.

The Difference Between Addiction And Dependence

The expressions ``habit" and "reliance" are frequently befuddled or utilized reciprocally. While there is some crossover, understanding the significant contrasts between the two is significant. A reliance is available when clients foster an actual resistance to a substance. They might encounter withdrawal side effects if they quit utilizing the drug. Typically a reliance is settled by leisurely tightening the utilization of a specific substance.

Then again, a habit happens when broad drug or liquor use has made an individual's cerebrum science change. Addictions manifest themselves as wild desires to utilize drugs, regardless of the mischief done to oneself or others. The best way to beat an addiction is through treatment.

Addiction And The Brain

Extreme substance misuse influences many pieces of the body, however, the organ most affected is the mind. At the point when an individual drinks a substance, for example, drug or liquor, the cerebrum creates a lot of dopamine; this triggers the mind's prize framework.

After rehashed drug use, the mind can't deliver ordinary measures of dopamine all alone. This implies dependent individuals might battle to find delight in pleasurable exercises, such as investing energy with companions or family when they are not affected by drugs or liquor.

On the off chance that you or a friend or family member is battling with a drug reliance, looking for treatment quickly is indispensable. Time after time individuals attempt to get better all alone, however, this can be troublesome and, now and again, perilous.

Myth About Addiction and recuperation

The very front of addiction and recuperation is immersed with obsolete and glaringly bogus data. Along these lines, there can be a great deal of disgrace and shame attached to the sickness of dependence, making it much more testing to recover. It is critical to discuss addiction straightforwardly and sincerely with the goal that not just the people who need treatment get the help they need, yet everyone around them can comprehend how to be a positive emotionally supportive network.

ADDICTION IS A CHOICE. THE USER COULD STOP IF THEY WANTED TO

This is most likely probably the greatest misconception. Driving experts on addiction concur that substance misuse is a persistent sickness like coronary illness, diabetes, and malignant growth. There is an assortment of variables that go into why somebody would battle with addiction. Life conditions like injury, psychological maladjustment, or hereditary qualities can contribute yet in some cases it doesn't have anything to do with it.

Addiction can happen to anybody. When dependence grabs hold, the mind science can change, making it hard to control driving forces. The substance turns into a desire, an addiction that can turn out to be a higher priority than different parts of life. The prize of dependence survives.

DRUG ADDICTS ARE BAD PEOPLE

Nobody intends to turn into an addict. Addiction itself can make somebody become an individual who takes more drugs, isn't accessible to companions or family, or goes with reckless decisions that they could not have possibly made in any case. However, they aren't a junkie since they were a terrible individual, they might turn into a terrible individual and settle on awful choices since they are addicts.

YOU CAN'T BE AN ADDICT IF YOU HOLD DOWN A TASK

At the point when many individuals picture an addict, they picture a messy, unkempt bum with no work or objectives throughout everyday life — one more generalization that society sustains. Many junkies work in normal life and might have exceptionally effective existences. Advanced fiends like this are seasoned veterans at covering their tracks so their compulsion slips by everyone's notice. This is particularly perilous because it makes it considerably harder for loved ones to mediate before it is past the point of no return.

YOU'D BE AWARE IF SOMEONE AROUND YOU WAS AN ADDICT

It's not generally as straightforward as you'd naturally suspect. As referenced above, there are loads of "advanced" addicts. Addiction accompanies a ton of culpability and shame so many foster ways of behaving that permit them to conceal their dependence, basically for a while.

Know the normal signs or ways of behaving that can show a habit, some include monetary issues, losing interest in things they once cherished, becoming disconnected or cryptic, and weight reduction and undesirable appearance. Realize that the illness of dependence is moderate and over the long haul it will just keep on deteriorating.

WHEN YOU RECEIVE TREATMENT YOUR JOURNEY WITH ADDICTION IS OVER

Addiction is a long-lasting interaction. Numerous people who have been clear for quite a long time tumble off the cart. It requires a steady exertion and unrestricted help to remain in front of the sickness.

ADDICTION IS A SIGN OF FAILURE

Addiction is a characteristic piece of the recuperation cycle. It doesn't, in any way, compare to disappointment. Whether you are recuperating from drugs, improving on any propensity can be hard. Having a psychological and actual reliance on something makes it substantially more troublesome.

LIQUOR ADDICTION ISN'T AS BAD AS DRUG ADDICTION

Liquor is adequate and effectively open; you might say it is praised in American culture. Millions participate in drinking as a social activity, and sadly this can be where liquor addiction begins.The social viewpoint makes the feeling that it is here and there less risky than drugs like heroin or cocaine yet the truth is, alcohol is a drug, a devastatingly lethal drug.

THERE IS A ONE TIME FIT ALL TREATMENT

There isn't anything that can supernaturally fix any habit. Everybody unexpectedly answers treatment, regardless of whether it is a similar substance being mishandled. An effective treatment ought to be customized to the individual and their particular necessities.

YOU SHOULD KEEP YOUR STRUGGLES WITH ADDICTION A SECRET

Many figure friends and family will think less about them, it will influence their status at work, or their companions will pass judgment on them for their addictions. However, this is all minuscule when it descends to your wellbeing and at last, the personal satisfaction you are living. Leaving well enough alone is immense mental weight and requires remarkable work to keep up with. Letting your loved ones see changes in you with next to no setting is troublesome on the two closures. Telling them going on makes the way for gainful help. Here and their individuals have significantly surprisingly compassion. Looking for help in any capacity is significant.

YOU MUST HIT THE ROCK BOTTOM TO HAVE A SUCCESSFUL RECOVERY

"Absolute bottom" shifts from one individual to another yet it's anything but essential for looking for treatment. Perceiving early that compulsion is going crazy is essential. Addiction doesn't just ease off; it will keep on rising until all in all nothing remains to be lost. However, it would be guileless to say it is as simple as perceiving the issue — and afterward ending it by looking for treatment.

Be that as it may, enabling a friend or family member to look for treatment might give them the inspiration they need. On the off chance that they aren't prepared to start treatment, they know about the choice. However, to find actual success, the individual going to treatment should be locked in and ready to change.

TENDING TO YOUR ADDICTION

On the off chance that you are worried about yourself or somebody you love, connect. Whether you are telling individuals interestingly or tending to somebody that has an issue, it requires to begin someplace. It will be awkward yet the flitting inconvenience doesn't measure up to the grave risks of a drawn-out habit. Be steady, and transparent both for you and the people around you. There is no time limit during the time spent recuperation, take it in steps. Everybody's process will be unique.

Phases Of Addiction

A habit doesn't shape precipitously for the time being. All things being equal, it is the consequence of a long course of rehashed substance misuse that bit by bit changes how a person sees drugs and how their body responds to it. This cycle is direct and has a similar movement for each individual, albeit the span of each progression in that movement can contrast significantly contingent upon the individual, measurement, and kind of drug being mishandled.

Since this interaction follows an example, it is feasible to separate it into the phases of a compulsion, beginning from an individual's most memorable use and driving the entire way to the habit itself.

The seven phases are:
Inception
Trial and error
Ordinary Usage
Dangerous Usage
Reliance
Habit
Emergency/Treatment

Seeing each stage and the ways of behaving related to each is an important method for distinguishing when somebody is in danger of fixation or has previously evolved one. As each stage advances so do the risks related to the medication's utilization, as the capacity to stop utilizing turns out to be significantly more troublesome.

Stage 1: Inception

The main phase of addiction is called inception, during which time the individual attempts a substance interestingly. This can occur at practically any time in an individual's life, most individuals with addictions attempted their drug decision before 18 and had a substance use jumble by 20. The reasons a youngster tries different things with drugs can change generally, yet two normal reasons are a direct result of one or the other interest or friend pressure. This last decision is made to attempt to fit in better with that specific gathering of companions.

Another explanation that young people are bound to attempt another drug than most age bunches is because of how the prefrontal cortex in their mind isn't yet totally created. This influences their dynamic cycle, and accordingly numerous youngsters settle on their decision without actually thinking about the drawn-out results of their activities. Since somebody has attempted a drug, it doesn't imply that they are sure to foster addiction. Much of the time, the individual removes a drug from interest, and afterward once that interest has been fulfilled, stops use.

This choice can likewise be affected by different elements connected with the drug's part in the individual's life, for example,

-Drug accessibility
-Peer use
-Family climate and medication history

-Emotional wellness (conditions like melancholy and tension frequently empower use)

Assuming conditions adjust and the individual keeps on taking the drug, they may before long end up in the second phase of compulsion.

Stage 2: Trial and error

At the trial and error stage, the client has moved past essentially giving the drug a shot on its own and is currently taking the medication in various settings to perceive what it means for their life. By and large, in this stage, the drug is associated with social activities, for example, encountering joy or unwinding following a monotonous day. For young people, it is utilized to improve party climates or oversee pressure from homework. Grown-ups for the most part enter trial and error either for delight or to battle pressure.

During Stage 2, there are next to zero desires for the drug; the individual will in any case go with a cognizant decision regardless of whether to utilize it. They might utilize it hastily or in a controlled way, and the recurrence of the two choices mostly relies upon an individual's temperament and justification behind utilizing the medication. There is no reliance as of now, and the individual can in any case stop the drug effects if they choose to.

Stage 3: Ordinary Usage

As an individual keeps on trying different things with a substance, its utilization becomes standardized and develops from occasional to ordinary use. This doesn't imply that they use it consistently, yet rather that there is some kind of example related to it.The example shifts given the individual, however, a couple of occurrences could be that they are taking it consistently or during times of close to home distress like dejection, weariness, or stress.

Right now, social clients might start taking their picked drug alone, thus removing the social component from their choice.The drug's utilization can likewise become dangerous right now and adversely affect the individual's life. For instance, the individual could start appearing for work hungover or high following an evening of drinking liquor or partaking in weed.

There is still no addiction as of now, yet the individual is probably going to consider their picked substance more regularly and may have started fostering a psychological dependence on it. At the point when this occurs, stopping becomes more earnestly, yet at the same time a sensible objective without outside help.

Stage 4: Dangerous Usage

With Stage 4, the singular's customary use has proceeded to develop and is presented as often as possible adversely affecting their lives. While an intermittent headache at work or an occasion is satisfactory for Stage 3, in Stage 4 cases like that become a standard event and its belongings become perceptible. The regular use may likewise prompt monetary hardships where there were none previously.

Albeit the client may not and by acknowledging it, individuals outwardly will more than likely notice a change in their way of behaving as of now. A portion of the normal changes to keep an eye out for in a drug addict include:

-Acquiring or taking cash
-Ignoring liabilities like work or family
-Endeavoring to conceal their drug use
-Concealing drugs in effectively open spots (like mint tins)
-Changing companion gatherings

-Visiting various specialists or quickly evolving specialists (if utilizing a professionally prescribed drug)
-Losing interest in old leisure activities

Stage 5: Reliance

The sign of entering Stage 5 is that an individual's drug use is at this point not sporting or clinical but instead is because of becoming dependent on the substance of the decision.This is at times seen as a wide stage that incorporates framing a resistance and reliance, however, at this point, the individual ought to as of now have fostered a resilience.Thus, this stage ought to just be set apart by a reliance, which can be physical, mental, or both.

For an actual reliance, the individual has manhandled their picked drug long enough that their body has adjusted to its presence and figured out how to depend on it. Assuming that utilization suddenly stops, the body will respond by entering withdrawal. This is described by a negative bounce back loaded up with awkward and at times perilous side effects, that ought to be overseen by clinical experts. Much of the time, people decide to proceed with their utilization, instead of looking for help, since it is the simplest and speediest method for getting away from withdrawal.

For certain drugs, particularly professionally prescribed meds, the individual might enter this stage through mental reliance before an actual one can shape.

At the point when this occurs, the individual accepts that they need the drug to have the option to work like a typical individual. Here, the drug normally turns into a way of dealing with hardship or stress for attempting times and afterward stretches out to cases where it shouldn't be important. For instance, a patient taking an aggravation prescription might start to over-sedate, as they see moderate torment as extreme agony.

Regardless, the singular takes the drug since they have come to a comprehension that they need it somehow or another to go on through life. When this attitude grabs hold, addiction is almost sure.

Stage 6: Habit

Reliance and addiction are words that are now and again utilized reciprocally, and however the words are comparable and habitually associated with drug use, they are unique.Probably the greatest distinction is that when an individual fosters a habit, their drug use is at this point, not a cognizant decision. Up until that point, it stays a sad remnant of one.

People at this stage feel like they can never again manage existence without admittance to their picked drug, and subsequently, lose unlimited oversight of their decisions and activities.The conduct moves that started during Stage 4 will develop to limits, with the client probably surrendering their old leisure activities and effectively keeping away from loved ones.

They may habitually lie about their drug use when addressed and are immediately upset assuming that their way of life is compromised in any capacity. Addicts, as of now, can likewise be so withdrawn from their previous lifestyle that they don't perceive how their ways of behaving are negative and the impacts that it has had on their connections.

Stage 7: Emergency/Treatment

The last phase of fixation is the limit in an individual's life. When here, the individual's addiction has developed far beyond their control and presently presents a genuine risk to their prosperity. It is at times alluded to as the emergency stage because as of now the fiend is at the most noteworthy gamble of experiencing a deadly excess or another sensational life occasion.

While an emergency is the worst situation imaginable for this stage, there is likewise a positive elective that fits here all things being equal. Either all alone or because of an emergency, this is when numerous people first track down help from a therapy clinic to start getting treatment.Thus, this stage can check the finish of their addiction, as well as the beginning of new existence without drug and alcohol, that is loaded up with trust for what's in store.

Diagnosing An Addiction

Diagnosing addiction resembles diagnosing some other ailment. The patient is analyzed by a clinical expert for side effects meeting explicit, logical models characterizing the sickness being referred to.

They include:

ABSENCE OF CONTROL

The substance is utilized in bigger sums or throughout a more drawn-out time than the individual initially expected. Those with dangerous substance use examples might feel like another person is picking their activities for them, and may end up doing whatever it may take to procure and utilize drugs without an overflow of cognizant consciousness of how they arrived.

WANT TO LIMIT USE

Addicts might need to scale back use however can't do such. They may over and again tell others and themselves that they anticipate endlessly stopping very soon at that. There can be a reasonable realization that abuse of substances isn't the so-called "right thing to do."

TIME SPENT

A lot of time is spent attempting to obtain a substance. The people who battle with addiction might design out how they will gain their ideal substance, spend quite a while executing their arrangement (particularly on the off chance that things turn out badly), and invest energy under the impacts of the substance — potentially weakened by its belongings and delayed consequences.

DESIRES

The addict encounters a profound longing or inclination to utilize the drug. Repeating contemplations of utilizing, or of the sentiments that one expects in the wake of utilizing, may happen at different focuses over the day or night. These can be extraordinarily unsavory and diverting.

ABSENCE OF RESPONSIBILITY

Substance use takes need over work, school, or home commitments. Days off might be utilized more regularly, plans might be made and afterward dropped without a second to spare, and there might be an assortment of reasons and defenses that are worried about outside conditions however are determined by habit.

ISSUES WITH RELATIONSHIP

Relational connections are reliably stressed from drug use. Companions might become distanced, attempting to help yet feeling uncertain of how to do as such. Relatives might feel a similar route; home life can endure, separation might happen, and psychosocial backing can lessen.

LOSS OF INTEREST

The addict quits taking part in significant social or sporting exercises for drug use. Similar to misery, there no longer is by all accounts any compensation in taking part in leisure activities or interests that once held enchantment.

RISKY USE

Use go on notwithstanding risky conditions. Addicts might wind up living in homes with different addicts, possibly sharing drugs gear in a way that might add to the illness. Inebriated driving can happen, which can end in death.

DEMOLISHING SITUATIONS

Use goes on regardless of deteriorated physical or mental issues. A descending winding might come to fruition; addicts might see the states of their lives weakening around them and conclude, what is happening, they should keep consuming drugs. This makes matters much more critical.

RESILIENCE

Bigger measures of the substance are expected to accomplish the ideal impacts. One or two beverages can become three or four, climbing upwards from that point. A joint can turn into a bong, which can transform into a touch. Dosages increment as the mind changes itself to the rehashed boosts it is being given trying to keep up with homeostasis.

WITHDRAWAL

This can be physical and profound. Incidental effects might incorporate uneasiness, peevishness, queasiness, and heaving. On account of serious liquor addiction, withdrawal might be deadly;

leading to a condition that can cause mental trips and seizures.

Cautioning Signs Of Addiction

Addictions start with trial and error with a substance. There are many reasons somebody could at first attempt a drug: interest, peer strain, stress, and issues at work or home are some of them. If you are concerned somebody you care about is battling with addiction, there are a few warnings you can search for. Be that as it may, it's memorable that everybody is unique; identifying addiction in certain individuals than in others might be more enthusiastic.

That being said, here are a few general admonition signs to know about:

-Overlooking responsibilities or obligations

-Issues at work, school, or home
-Unexplained non attendances
-Seeming to have another arrangement of companions
-Impressive financial vacillations
-Changes in rest design
-Slips in focus or memory
-Being strangely clandestine about pieces of individual life
-Withdrawal from typical social contacts
-Abrupt emotional episodes and changes in conduct
-Surprising absence of inspiration
-Weight reduction or changes in actual appearance

Chapter 2: ADDICTION AND RELATIONSHIP

ADDICTION AND RELATIONSHIP

At The Point When Someone You Love Has an Addiction

The aftermath of a habit, for fiends and individuals who love them, is destroying - the controls, the responsibility, the obliteration of connections, and the breakage of individuals. At the point when junkies realize they are cherished by somebody who has put resources into them, they promptly have fuel for their addiction.

Your adoration and your need to bring them securely through their compulsion could see you giving the cash you can't manage, saying OK when that yes will annihilate you, deceiving, safeguarding them, and having your body divert cold with dread from the noon ring of the telephone.

You could quit preferring them, however, you don't quit adoring them. If you're trusting that the junkie will stop the madness - the fits of remorse, the lying, the control - it won't work out. If you can't express no to the controls of their addiction in your unaddicted state, realize that they won't express no from their dependent one. Not because they will not, but since they can't.

Assuming that you love an addict, it will be long and unbearable before you understand that there is nothing you can do. It will come when you're depleted, shattered, and when you feel the aggravation of their implosion squeezing persistently and for all time against you. The connections and your general surroundings will begin to break, and you'll cut yourself into spiked pieces. That is the point at which you'll be aware, from the most profound and most flawless piece of you, that you can't live like this any longer.

I've worked with a lot of addicts, however, the words in this post come from cherishing one. I have somebody in my life who has been dependent on different substances. It's been deplorable to watch. It's been considerably more grievous to watch the impact on my loved ones who are nearer to him than I am. I would lie assuming I said that my sympathy has been undying. It hasn't. It's been depleted and stripped back to uncovered. I feel routine like I have nothing passed on to give him.

What I've realized, after numerous years, is that there is nothing anybody can do to transform him. With the entirety of our consolidated insight, strength, love, and unfailing will to improve things for him, there is no other option for us.

I understood some time prior that I was unable to ride in the front seat with somebody in the driver's seat who was on a particularly persevering way to implosion. It's required numerous years, a ton of bitterness, and a great deal of inadvertent blowback to individuals, connections, and lives beyond his. What I can be sure of is that when he is prepared to take a different path, I'll be there, with affection, empathy, and a wild obligation to remain next to him in the manner he wants to help his recuperation. He will have a multitude of individuals behind him and close to him when he goes with the choice, however up to that point, I and other people who love him are frail. That's what I know.

No one expects a way of behaving to turn into a habit, and if you are somebody who cherishes a junkie - whether it's a parent, kid, accomplice, companion, or kin - the responsibility, the disgrace, and the weakness can overpower. Dependence isn't a sickness of character, character, soul, or situation. It can happen to anybody. It's a human condition with human results and being that we as a whole are human, we are in general powerless.

Fiends can emerge from any life and from any family. Almost certainly, in the course of our life, on the off chance that we don't cherish somebody with a dependence, we'll know somebody who does, so this is a significant discussion to have, for us all.

The issue with adoring a friend is that occasionally the things that will help them are the things that would appear to be harmful, cold, and savage assuming they were finished in light of non-addicts. Frequently, the most ideal ways to answer a fiend have the amazing ability to suffocate the people who love them with responsibility, melancholy, self-question, and obviously, obstruction.

Adoring a junkie in any way can be one of the loneliest places on the planet. It's not difficult to feel determined to pull out help for the junkie, however, at last, this turns into the main conceivable reaction.

Except if somebody has been in a fight covering next to you, battling the battle, being pushed to the brink of collapse, with their heartbroken and their will tried, it's not so much for them to pass judgment. The more we can discuss transparent addiction,the more we can lift the disgrace, responsibility, pain, and steadfast self-question that frequently holds up traffic of having the option to answer a fiend such that upholds their mending, as opposed to their addiction. It's by talking that we give each other consent to feel what we feel, love who we love, and be what our identity is, with the weaknesses, frayed edges, fortitude, and intelligence that are every one of them a piece of being human.

When Someone You Love is an Addict

You're managing somebody different at this point

At the point when a habit grabs hold, the individual you love vanishes, basically until the dependence relaxes its grasp. The individual you love is still in there someplace, however that is not who you're managing. The individual you recall might have been warm, entertaining, liberal, astute, solid - such countless great things - yet addiction changes individuals. A significant chunk of time must pass to conform to this reality and it's exceptionally common to answer the dependent individual like the individual in question is the individual you recall.

This makes it so natural to succumb to the controls, the untruths, and the treachery - again and again. You're answering the individual you recollect - however, this isn't that individual. The sooner you're ready to acknowledge this, the sooner you can begin working for the individual you love and recollect, which will mean doing what in some cases feels horrible, and continuously sad, so the addiction is famished of the ability to fend for that individual off.

The individual you love is in there - support that individual, not the fiend before you. The sooner you're ready to quit succumbing to the controls, falsehoods, disgrace, and culpability that takes care of their compulsion, the more probable it will be that the individual you recollect will want to track down the way back to you.Try not to anticipate that they should be on your rationale. At the point when a dependence grabs hold, the individual's world becomes twisted by that fixation. Comprehend that you can't prevail upon them or convince them to see things how you do.

As far as they might be concerned, their untruths don't feel like falsehoods. Their disloyalty doesn't feel like double-crossing. Their implosion doesn't necessarily feel like an implosion. It seems like endurance. The change will come when there is no other choice except to change, not when you're ready to track down the switch by giving them enough data or rationale. While you're safeguarding them from their aggravation, you're disrupting the general flow of their motivation to stop.

Fiends will successfully take care of their addiction since when the fixation isn't there, the profound aggravation that occupies the space is more prominent. Individuals will possibly change when what they are doing causes them enough torment, that changing is a preferred choice over remaining something very similar. That is not only for friends, that is for us all. We frequently stay away from change - connections, occupations, propensities - until we've felt sufficient uneasiness with the old circumstance, to open up to an alternate choice.

Change happens when the power for change is more prominent than the power to remain something very similar. Until the aggravation of the enslavement offsets the close-to-home agony that drives the addiction, there will be no change. At the point when you accomplish something that makes their habit-forming conduct more straightforward or shields them from the aggravation of their dependence - maybe by crediting them cash, lying for them, driving them around - you're preventing them from arriving where they feel sufficient torment that relinquishing the addiction is a superior choice. Try not to limit the habit, overlook it, rationalize it or cover it up. Love them, however, don't hold up traffic of their recuperating by safeguarding them from the aggravation of their compulsion.

What It's Like Loving An Addict

The experience of cherishing a junkie can be marginally unique for everybody, except there are a few general shared characteristics that the vast majority say they experience. To start with, when you love a friend, you need to comprehend that their habit outweighs all the other things, including you.

Individuals can begin to think about it literally, and it justifiably harms them profoundly to feel as though the fiend they love just thinks often about the drug's or liquor, yet the junkie's mind is driving them toward setting the substance at the highest point of their need list. Regardless of what a junkie says or guarantees, they are just determined by their longing to keep utilizing, and there's not a lot of anything you can do to change that.

Additionally, when you love a junkie, they will lie, cheat and take to get what they need, which is more drugs or liquor. They can be enchanting and manipulative when it fills their needs, and as the adored one of a fiend, it's fundamental that you comprehend that it is just only that: control. At the point when you love a junkie, you may continually feel that you're nervous, or stressed when that feared call will come.

So how could you at any point respond when you love a junkie?

There's little you can do, and you positively can't fix the individual. Addiction is a complicated illness, and there's no measure of undermining or asking that will kill the issue. All things being equal, probably everything you can manage when you love a junkie is ensuring you're not empowering them. Empowering a fiend alludes to ways of behaving or situations where you're eliminating outcomes from the ways of behaving of the junkie. It very well may be essentially as basic as lying for the individual or covering for them.

Whenever you've recognized how you are empowering the junkie, you can begin defining limits and blueprint results. Then, one of the main genuine moves you can initiate to help an addict is to set up for them to go to treatment.

Indications Of Addiction In A Relationship

A few couples know before they say "I do" that a partner dislikes drugs or liquor. Those in recuperation can be the best, most composed individuals you'll meet, however they can likewise backslide. Different couples might be stunned to figure out the degree of a partner's concerns with drugs or alcohol. Junkies can be particularly adept at hiding their concerns from others, and that incorporates their companion or likely life partner.

It might very well be solely after you're hitched that you understand your partner has a substance misuse issue, and afterward the entirety of your consideration goes to aiding your dependent companion. For yet a third gathering, addiction creeps into the marriage. One partner goes through a medical procedure and takes important solution pain relievers during recuperation, just to find they can't quit taking them. Somebody starts to fiddle with marijuana, cocaine, or engineered drugs. After-work stops at the bar become daily occasions rather than week-by-week occasions. It doesn't make any difference how your accomplice got where they are today. What is more important rather is perceiving the issue, and understanding and carrying out the dos and don'ts of aiding your dependent companion.

Perceiving Signs Of Substance Use Disorder In A Relationship

Each couple is one of a kind, and the indications of drug and liquor misuse might be hard to detect or plain to see. On the off chance that you suspect your partner has an issue, search for the accompanying signs and side effects:

-Cash vanishing without clarification.
-Medications, liquor, or medication stuff concealed around the house.

-Broad time spent "with companions" celebrating, particularly without you.

-Broken guarantees, for example, a vow not to drink at a party that transforms into a gorge.

-Failure to quit drinking or utilizing substances even after rehashed vows not to utilize them.

-Driving while inebriated or impaired.

-Seriously endangering kids' or others' lives with their inebriation or conduct while inebriated.

-Investing more energy away from home without clarification.

-Trouble keeping a task, particularly because of persistent delay or non-attendance.

-Medical problems, for example, liver issues, bruises that will not recuperate, persistent hacks, or stomach-related issues.

Numerous companions say they feel like a solitary parent when their accomplice goes on medications or liquor. Perhaps the hardest thing to bear while your cherished one is utilizing is the excessive weight it puts on you to run the family while your partner battles with their infection. Drugs and liquor can definitely make individuals' characters change. While impaired or while encountering desires, they might say or do things they wouldn't regularly do. Character changes are difficult for a mate. Maybe the individual you wedded or in love with has vanished, supplanted by a beast named Addiction.

The Don't Of Dealing With An Addicted Spouse

Notwithstanding this rundown of do's, there's likewise a rundown of don'ts while managing a dependent companion.

To help your dependent companion, don't:

-Lie for your mate: Lying to cover your partner's headache or gorge won't assist with getting them into recuperation quicker. Try not to phone in wiped out for your partner or rationalize to family or companions for an odd way of behaving. Allow your companion to make sense of and assume liability.

-Conceal their habit: Hiding pill bottles, alcohol contains, or in any case covering for your life partner's addiction simply assists them with proceeding with a similar way they're on. Try not to cover their tracks.

-Stay away from the issue: Many accomplices choose to disregard their life partner's dependence out of fear. They might be hesitant to confront the outcomes or even apprehensive things will change. The old maxim "Satan you know is superior to the one you don't have any idea about" guides many individuals into waiting in terrible circumstances as opposed to looking for help.

Try not to overlook your partner's concerns. Assuming your life partner had chest torments, you'd demand they go to the trauma center. If your companion is battling with addiction, you'll likewise have to make a move and assist them with finding a recuperation program. Disregarding it won't make it disappear.

-Use drugs or drink to stay with them: Using close your life partner for an organization doesn't assist them with getting off of drugs or liquor and may simply energize their awful way of behaving. More awful, you might wind up dependent, as well.

-Fault or judge: When you become familiar with current realities about compulsion, you'll comprehend addiction is an infection. Faulting and passing judgment on your companion for their activities doesn't help. It just makes them get some distance from you. Odds are great they need to quit ingesting medications or drinking, yet they simply don't have any idea how. Tackles settle nothing.

-Get some distance from your companion: Even on the off chance that you need to move out for a brief time, stay in touch with your life partner. Dismissing or keeping them out of your life ought to be a final hotel held for individuals who become fierce or oppressive.

- Fault yourself: It is never your shortcoming that your accomplice battles with addiction. Hereditary qualities, social variables, and, indeed, family elements can impact habit. In any case, a definitive decision to drink or take drugs was with your companion. Sooner or later, the capacity to pick is lost as habit grabs hold. Your mate decided to take that first beverage or fiddle with it for quite a while. You're not to fault for their way of behaving.

-Anticipate that things should get back to what they were: Even after your mate enters recuperation, your life and your relationship will never get back to what it was. That happens regardless of the major two or three faces, whether it's a disease, a respiratory failure, or an addiction. Acknowledge that your relationship is on another balance, and realize what this implies as you both leave on your mate's program of recuperation.

The Most Effective Method To Help A Spouse With Drug Addiction: Finding Harmony

Assuming your partner consents to enter treatment, this is the very thing you can anticipate:

Contingent upon what sort of dependence your accomplice battles with, they might have to enter a detox program. During detox, individuals are checked to ensure their well being stays protected while their bodies free themselves of drugs and alcohol. Your partner might remain at a treatment office where the person in question will go to gatherings or individual directing, recuperation gatherings, and different projects to advance recuperation.
You'll cooperate to make a diagram for recuperation.

An outline records the means your partner needs to take to remain solid and liberated from drugs or liquor. You'll track down ways of supporting, empowering, and helping your partner stay perfect and sober. Your partner might require a lot of chances to go to recuperation gatherings or converse with backers or program companions. It's normal for the non-dependent partner to understand. To start with, dependence removes a ton of family time, and presently it appears like recuperation requires something very similar or greater investment away. Assuming that it becomes hazardous for you, inquire as to whether you can go to start gatherings together where family participation is empowered.

One more supportive method for building areas of strength is to make a set timetable for family time when your partner can focus on hanging out to adjust the time spent in recuperation. Know that while things won't return to how they were, they can improve. Once in a while, they even beat them before addiction turned into an issue.

There's A Different Way To Love An Addict

At the point when you love them how you adored them before the addiction, you can wind up supporting the habit, not the individual. Solid limits are significant for both of you. The limits you once had could find you honestly doing things that make it more straightforward for the addiction to proceed. It's alright to express no to things you could have once consented to - as a matter of fact, it's fundamental - and is many times one of the most cherishing things you can do.

On the off chance that it's troublesome, have an anchor - an expression or a picture to help you to remember why your 'no' is so significant. If you feel like saying no endangers you, the dependence has immovably implanted itself into the existence of the individual you love. In these conditions, be available to the likelihood that you might require proficient help to assist you with remaining safe, maybe by halting contact. Keeping a distance between you both is no reflection of how much love and responsibility you feel to the individual, and about keeping you both safe.

YOUR BOUNDARIES

They're significant for both of you. If you love a fiend, your limits will frequently be grounded and higher than they are with others in your life. It's not difficult to feel disgrace and responsibility around this, however, realize that your limits are significant because they'll be buckling down for both of you.

Defining limits will assist you with seeing things all the more obviously from all points since you will not be as dazed by the wreck or as able to see things through the junkie's eyes - a view that frequently includes qualification, sadness, and putting stock the legitimacy of their manipulative way of behaving. Put down your stopping points affectionately and as frequently as the need might arise. Be clear about the results of disregarding the limits and ensure you finish, generally, it's mistaken for the fiend and unreasonable for everybody.

Imagining that your limits aren't significant will see the fiend's way of behaving deteriorate as your limits get more slender. In the end, this will just damage both of you. You can't fix them, and it's significant for everybody that you quit attempting.
The fiend and what they do are unchangeable as far as you might be concerned. They generally will be. A dependence is all-consuming and it mutilates reality. Know the contrast between what you can transform (you, how you think, the things you do) and what you can't transform (any other person).

There will be a strength that comes from this, yet accepting this will require some investment, and that is not a problem. Assuming you love somebody who has an addiction, realize that their halting isn't simply a question of needing to. Relinquish expecting to fix them or change them and deliver them with adoration, for the well-being of you and theirs.

SEE THE REALITY

At the point when dread becomes overpowering, forswearing is a truly typical method for shielding yourself from a difficult reality. It's simpler to imagine that all is well, yet this will just permit the habit-forming conduct to cover itself more profoundly. Pay heed assuming you are being approached to give cash, close to home assets, time, and looking after children anything over feels great. Pay to heed likewise of the inclination, but there's something off about weak, that something. Sentiments are strong, and will by and large attempt to alarm us when there's something wrong with something, well before our brains will tune in.

DON'T DO THINGS THAT KEEP THEIR ADDICTION ALIVE

At the point when you love a junkie, a wide range of limits and shows get obscured. Realize the contrast between aiding and empowering. Helping considers the drawn-out impacts, advantages, and results. Empowering is tied in with giving quick alleviation, and neglects the drawn-out harm that could accompany that momentary help.

Giving cash, convenience, dropping sound limits to oblige the junkie - these are le with regards to taking care of somebody you love, however with somebody who has an addiction, it's assisting with keeping the addiction alive.

BE AS HONEST AS YOU CAN ABOUT THE IMPACT OF YOUR CHOICES

This is so troublesome - I know how troublesome this is, yet when you change what you do, the junkie will likewise need to change how the person obliges those changes.This will probably turn you into responsibility, however, let the dependent one in on that when the person in question chooses to do things any other way, you'll be the first there and your arms will be open, and that you love them however much you at any point have.

You will probably hear that you're not accepted, however, this is intended to refuel your empowering conduct. Get what they are talking about, be disheartened by it, and feel remorseful assuming you need to - yet for the good of them, don't alter your perspectives.

TRY NOT TO BUY INTO THEIR VIEWS OF THEMSELVES

Fiends will accept with all aspects of their being that they can't exist without their addiction. Try not to get involved with it. They can be entire without their dependence however they will have a hard time believing it, so you'll want to trust it enough for both of you. You would need to acknowledge that they aren't prepared to move towards that yet, and that is OK, yet meanwhile don't effectively uphold their perspective on themselves as having no choice except completely to their addiction.

Each time you accomplish something that upholds their addiction, you're imparting your absence of confidence in their ability to live without it. Let that be an anchor that keeps your limits solid.

WHEN YOU STAND YOUR GROUND, THINGS MIGHT GET WORSE BEFORE THEY GET BETTER

The more you permit yourself to be controlled, the more you will be controlled. At the point when you persevere and quit surrendering to the control, the manipulation might deteriorate before it stops. When something that has consistently worked quits working, it's human instinct to do it more. Try not to surrender to lying, accusing, or manipulating. They might pull out, rage, become profoundly miserable, or foster torment or ailment. They'll stop when they understand your determination, however, you'll be the first to conclude that what they're accomplishing won't work any longer.

YOU AND SELF LOVE, IT'S A NECESSITY

Similarly, that it's the junkie's responsibility to recognize their necessities and meet them in safe and satisfying ways, you additionally should distinguish and meet your own. Any other way you will be depleted and harmed - inwardly, genuinely, and profoundly, and that is not great for anybody.

WHAT ARE YOU GETTING OUT OF IT?

This is a hard inquiry and will take an open, valiant heart to investigate it. Junkies utilize habit-forming ways of behaving to prevent feeling torment. Justifiably, individuals who love them frequently utilize empowering ways of behaving to likewise prevent feeling torment. It is appalling to Love a junkie. Assisting the individual with canning is a method for facilitating your aggravation and can feel like a method for stretching out affection to somebody you're frantic to reach. It can likewise be a method for making up for the terrible sentiments you could feel towards the individual for the aggravation they cause you.

This is all truly typical, yet it's essential to investigate how you may be accidentally adding to the issue. Tell the truth, and be prepared for troublesome things to come up. Do it with a confided face-to-face or an instructor on the off chance that you help. It very well may be one of the main things you can accomplish for the junkie. Ponder what you envision will occur on the off chance that you quit doing how you're doing them.Then, at that point, contemplate what will occur on the off chance that you don't. What you're doing could save the individual temporarily, yet the more extraordinary the habit-forming conduct, the more disastrous the definitive results of that way of behaving if it's permitted to proceed.

You can't stop it from proceeding, yet you can quit adding to it. See how you're doing with an open heart, and be adequately valiant to challenge yourself on anything that you could be doing that is keeping the addiction alive.The more straightforward you make it for them to keep up with their addiction, the simpler it is for them to keep up with their dependence. It's as basic, and as muddled, like that.

WHAT CHANGES DO YOU NEED TO MAKE IN YOUR OWN LIFE?

Zeroing in on a fiend is probably going to imply that the emphasis on your own life has been turned down - a ton. In some cases, zeroing in on the fiend is a method for keeping away from the aggravation of managing different issues that can hurt you. At the point when you investigate this, be thoughtful to yourself, generally, the allurement will be to keep on dulling the truth. Be daring, and be delicate and reconstruct your identity, your limits, and your life. You can't anticipate that the fiend in your life should manage their issues, mend, and take the hugely bold action towards building a solid life assuming you are reluctant to do that for yourself.

TRY NOT TO BLAME THE ADDICT

The fiend could merit a ton of the fault, however, fault will keep you irate, hurt, and feeble. Fixation is as of now vigorously saturated with disgrace. The fuel began it and the fuel will push it along. Be cautious you're not adding to keeping the disgrace fire lit.

SHOW RESTRAINT

Go for progress, not flawlessness. There will be forward advances and a lot of other ones as well. Try not to consider a retrogressive advance to be a disappointment. It's not. Recuperation never occurs in a flawless forward line and reverse advances are all important for the cycle

HERE AND THERE, YOU ONLY HAVE TO LET GO

Once in a while, all the adoration on the planet isn't sufficient. Cherishing somebody with a compulsion can tear at the creases of your spirit. It can feel that difficult. Assuming you've never experienced it, relinquishing somebody you love profoundly, could appear to be inconceivable yet on the off chance that you're approaching that point, you'll know the distress and the profundity of crude agony that can drive such an incomprehensible choice.

Per adventure you want to give up, realize that this is not a problem. In some cases it's the main choice. Relinquishing somebody doesn't mean you quit adoring them - it never intends that. You can in any case leave the way open assuming you need to. Indeed, even at their most frantic, most demolished, most forsaken point, let them in on that you have faith in them and that you'll be there when they're prepared to accomplish something else. This will leave the way open, however, will place the obligation regarding their recuperating in their grasp, which is the main spot for it to be.

Steps To Take When Helping an Addict or Alcoholic Partner

To assist you to collaborate with recuperating from Substance Use Disorder or liquor addiction, a decent initial step is to learn all that you can about addiction and the treatment choices accessible.The more you know about the thing he is managing, the better prepared you will be to offer help. While managing an addiction dependent partner, you should acknowledge you can't drive them to recuperate. Nonetheless, there are a few things you can do to urge them to maintain that should do such, yet the decision to look for a clearheaded life is at last theirs

It is critical to be straightforward with yourself and with them about their habits and conduct. Tell them what it is meaning for you, yet just address your experience. This implies utilizing "I" explanations, for example, "I feel frightened when you become inebriated and I don't have the foggiest idea where you are." Stay cool and be cautious with your tone and language so they do not feel left behind. Be all around as sympathetic and steady as could act, while likewise being firm about your sentiments.

Express veritable love and concern as opposed to finding faults.Recollect that you don't need to act like a lone ranger while attempting to help your dependent partner. Look for the assistance of loved ones, and think about organizing a gathering intercession if they are not responsive to your ideas.

Things To Avoid When Helping An Addict or Alcoholic Partner

With regards to aiding your dependent partner, or anybody you love who is engaging in an addiction, knowing what not to do is similarly all around as significant as understanding what to do. Here are things to keep away from while attempting to help your dependent partner :

-Try not to utilize responsibility, fault, disgrace, or other pessimistic feelings. This will just make them guarded and less receptive to your ideas.

-Try not to empower their way of behaving. You can help them, yet don't empower them. At the point when you empower, you remove the normal, unfortunate results of their habit-forming conduct, making it more straightforward for them to utilize.

-Stay away from ultimatums, they don't work. Some may be enticed to say, "I'll leave you on the off chance that you don't stop drugs," yet this approach frequently misfires and might add to the burdens previously looked at by your partner and makes a final proposal circumstance that many view as difficult to finish.

All things being equal, put down solid stopping points — yet just the ones you are ready to adhere to. Also, make the limits about what is best for you, as opposed to providing your capacity to them. For instance: "If I think you've been drinking, I won't invest energy with you." This way, you are not defining the limit on whether they believe they are alcoholic, however, whether you do. It places you steering the ship of safeguarding your limits.

-Try not to contend with them or endeavor to discuss their fixation when they are impaired. They can likely not have a normal discussion, and may not recollect it the following day. On the off chance that you can find the open door, hold on until they are level-headed to have significant conversations.

-Try not to go along with them. Try not to allow their addiction to impact you and influence you in a comparative way. Hold your ground and keep up with your temperance paying little mind to what they are doing.

The Most Effective Method to Let Go Of An Addict You Love

You might come to a point in your life where you need to relinquish a junkie you love.

This is frequently after they've been denied treatment, or kept on utilizing drugs despite endeavors to make limits and outcomes. Sadly, figuring out how to relinquish a junkie you love is a lot more difficult than one might expect.There are few stages you can take whenever you have concluded the opportunity has arrived to relinquish a fiend you love.

To begin with, you should isolate yourself, both actually and inwardly. During this time, you should find areas of strength for a framework since you will require it. Frequently friends and family of a fiend will partake in a gathering of others whose friends and family are junkies. At the point when you do that it can assist you with pushing ahead in a positive, useful way, and furthered that you're in good company. During this time you will likewise have to make a rundown of things that you realize you should change as a feature of your objective of relinquishing a fiend you love.

If portions of the responsibilities you make to yourself during this time, it's OK, can keep pushing ahead without being too unforgiving with yourself. What's generally significant as you figure out how to relinquish a junkie you love is basically to give your all. You ought to likewise attempt to find things that you appreciate accomplishing for yourself, and you ought to chip away at making your desired existence without the incorporation of the fiend.

At long last, while you're investigating how to relinquish a fiend you love, as hard as it could be you need to relinquish dread. Cherishing a fiend frequently implies that you're tormented with consistent trepidation, and that can lead you to feel discouraged or irredeemable. You need to attempt to deal with relinquishing those sentiments and dealing with yourself while pushing ahead.

Recuperation Is A Family Project

Consider recuperation a family project. You'll find there are useful projects for the partners of recuperating junkies and your youngsters. Finding a recuperation place that incorporates relatives as a component of the arrangement for recuperation is likewise significant. While those battling with substance are answerable for their habit, there can be relational intricacies that increment the chances of addiction. Being in recuperation together, regardless of whether you're not effectively dependent, can assist you with mending mental injuries that might be keeping you down, as well.

Conclusion

Adoring a fiend is one of the most troublesome things that can happen to a person. Whether you're in a heartfelt connection with a junkie, or it's your youngster, parent, or another person you're near, keeping on cherishing somebody with a dependence on medications or alcohol is unquestionably troublesome. While you might put forth your best attempt to help them, sooner or later, you could likewise need to comprehend how to relinquish a fiend you love.

Usually, it's not unexpected to assist our loved ones when they need it, however, there is a distinction between aiding and empowering. Aiding upholds the individual. Empowering upholds the compulsion. However, what marriage isn't difficult to work? Anything valuable merits getting along admirably, and anything advantageous requires exertion. Marriage isn't unique. Indeed, even in the best relationships, things can turn out badly.

Printed in Great Britain
by Amazon